"Poem after brilliant poem bears witness to the collapse of the boundaries between her body and the land that surrounds it. Like the river winding through this book, Schmuhl remakes herself before our eyes. *Premonitions* is a reminder that in our modern era of distraction, our bodies always have a place in the world of ten thousand things."

—Tomás Q. Morín, author of *Patient Zero*

"*Premonitions* accumulates a haunting record of a speaker subsumed into the necessary madness of nature, a nature whose cycles of proliferation and death, the rhythms of day and night and those of the seasons, constitute a psychic and bodily drama staggeringly rendered through Schmuhl's lyric voice. These are poems of isolation and the spirit of place, and there is no question that they make an important contribution to the regional literatures of the Midwest as well as the vibrant canons of contemporary poetry and lyric prose at large."

—Ryo Yamaguchi, author of *The Refusal of Suitors*

"*Premonitions* is a collection by a poet we've waited to read, and who's both come to us in these meditations softly and with unforgettable force. Elizabeth Schmuhl is a poet of deceptive subtlety, so this is a book one will return to over and over again—as one does to each line and each page— to discover further depths, to re-appreciate an image, to be startled by the power of these musical discoveries. Like songs, like spells, like prayers, like ghosts glimpsed in the corner of an eye, we are alarmed and charmed and changed by this poetry. This poet has transformed experience into substance and then transformed that substance into breath and dream. This collection is the debut of an important new voice."

—Laura Kasischke, author of *The Infinitesimals*

PREMONITIONS

MADE IN MICHIGAN WRITERS SERIES

GENERAL EDITORS

Michael Delp, Interlochen Center for the Arts
M. L. Liebler, Wayne State University

A complete listing of the books in this series can
be found online at wsupress.wayne.edu

PREMONITIONS

Poems by Elizabeth Schmuhl

WAYNE STATE UNIVERSITY PRESS
DETROIT

ISBN 978-0-8143-4498-9 (paperback)
ISBN 978-0-8143-4499-6 (e-book)

Library of Congress Control Number: 2017960707

Publication of this book was made possible by a generous gift from The Meijer Foundation. This work is supported in part by an award from the Michigan Council for Arts and Cultural Affairs.

Wayne State University Press
Leonard N. Simons Building
4809 Woodward Avenue
Detroit, Michigan 48201–1309

Visit us online at wsupress.wayne.edu

#7

I stopped using the internet years ago. All of the places I wanted to go weren't there. Now the fig. Now the peach. And when I want to be away from the orchard, I go to the river and the river feeds me.

Some days I miss the web and start feeling low. I go to the barn where the air is thick with straw and heat. I climb the ladder to the swallow nests.

I dance until sweat turns my tank top transparent, until my underwear clings to my thighs. My sweat evaporating, turning me more into me, disappearing.

#9

I'm getting better at not doubting myself.

The fish from the river that cuts through this place
are swimming through my veins.

That's impossible, he says, looking out the window at the moon.

I am going to slice myself open to show you, I say, smiling.

He turns back and scowls, *I'll leave the second you do.*

I grab a knife and split myself open.

Their silver bodies are rushing in a stream, pooling onto the floor.

*I thought I felt scales brushing against the walls of my
vascular system, and I was right,* I say enthusiastically, looking
at the fresh wound.

I go outside, smoke twelve of the fish over an open fire. Their bodies
dry into the shape of leaves still hanging on peach trees past September.

In a large triangle, I arrange them on the lawn. Their eyes shine back the sharp light of distant stars, the closer moon.

I dream of an orchard and the fish are there to greet me. *Thank you*, they say. *We didn't think you'd come this soon.*

#14

In the cherry orchard I offer myself to the Earth.
She takes me.

I sink easily. My blood sweet and salty, staining
the loamy ground.

Clouds move like field mice through a deep purple sky.

Slowly, I arrive.

#15

As a spirit, find me
raking the orchard sand
with my long fingers.

If you discover an arrowhead
know I saw it first.

Any petals that have floated
from fruit trees
have already fallen
on my head.

I shake them
out of my hair
while dancing
to the evening
sounds slowly
turning on.

You're welcome
anytime to watch.

#17

I'm in a white dress. It's dirty.

I go for walks in the peach orchard and pretend the trees are my friends.
The pretending doesn't seem like pretending.

I'm wet and salty, and when I feel my skin burning, I walk home.
I'm dirtier than before. Look at my nails. I'm hungry.

Inside the farmhouse the air is cool. The water I pour myself is cooler.

I drink it at the oak table and smoke. I don't eat because I know
if I hold off, I will get drunk quicker later.

I stare out the bay window at the elm leaves. There's wind.

#18

The yolky sun is cracking as the waves inside me thicken.

Do you think you'll ever go missing? he asks.

My sails are steady and blue.

Look how they're clustered, I say. *Watch how elegantly they move.*

I would miss you, he says.

Don't you already?

He says, *Do you think you'll ever return?*

#22

Close your eyes:
shore or forest?

How can you even be sure?

Time has a way of
allowing these kinds of questions
to ripen, to surface.

I'm lonely living
in this sea of leaves.

#24

The snow is beautiful and I want to die. Who could
refuse this softness?

Not the plants or their petals: lost memories.
Or their limbs: tiny skeletons.

I have given myself permission to lie down forever.
It's a miracle: today, the Earth has even made me this bed.

#25

This morning the trees
may as well be mountains

I am here and nowhere
all at once

My lungs branch and
so do the maple's

rivers cutting through
all of my valleys please

pass me a cigarette
let me put myself out

#26

Beetles in
the hydrangeas
at night.

I kneel
waiting
till dawn.

Not even
a moth
has landed
on one of
my petals.

The earth here
acidic. The
hydrangeas
no longer
pink.

#27

The fox visited me for one week, then stopped coming.

Each night, she told me, *I dug a hole on the banks of the river.*

I'm sorry, I'd say, *I'm not ready.*

If a fox appeared and asked me to join her, I'd say okay and go willingly, I think.

#29

Put a raspberry between your lips.
Press down.
Sip in its sweet tenderness.
That's me.

#31

The basement is cool and smells like wet cement and dead insects. I am barefoot and walk into the laundry room where the cellar used to be.

In the sand floor, I dig with my toes. Above: spiderwebs. Egg sacks haphazardly strung on them like pearls.

There is no mirror here but I know what I look like. Broken.

I braid my hair and hope for the eggs to split open, for life to crawl out.

#34

It is night. I drink red wine and become pregnant with
an old lover's baby. I dance, knife in hand, and at my
movement's climax, stab my belly. I feel no pain. Instead
I feel ecstatic.

Upstairs, I'm in bed with the lights off. Smoking in the center of
my dirty dress. I am my dirty dress.

I listen to the coyotes howl on the distant tracks. They are calling
to far off trains. Come. An ancestor approaches and kisses my ear,
strokes my hair. Puts my cigarette out.

#37

A bloody womb and all I can think of
are the turkey vultures. Their large bodies
perched awkwardly on the barn's spine.

They stay four days until
my bed linens are in full bloom.

The scent is suffocating.

Without warning, the birds fly through my window, break the glass,
enter.

It smells, they say.

I know. Please take me to the river.

They laugh, *You're too heavy.*

But this is a dream. I say, *You can lift me.*

On the banks of the Paw Paw
the wet mud wakes me.

I never want to go back to the farmhouse to clean myself.
Never again do I want to belong to a room.

#39

the snow of yesterday
that fell like cherry petals
is water once again *
and I drink it as I walk
down the dirt road
to an opening in the forest.

My body is just a vehicle
to move me so I leave it
here, on the dirt floor.

I return several days later
moss growing
all over my throat.

Doesn't my voice sound
different, lovely
when I sing with the owl
to the harvest moon?

*Haiku by Gozan, 18th century

#40

Everything on this farm is
so hungry the orchards
filled with swallows swooping
gorging at high noon

I watch them until evening
until the breeze cuts
through us until crickets
blink like stars like remnants
of the heavens we both once were

#43

I bite into a peach and understand
why you want so violently.

#44

He comes to see me.

In the raspberry patch he says, *I would like to eat your hair.*

I laugh.

Can I cut some? he asks.

I hold up a lock from the front. I should have held up one from the back because for months, I will look at myself in the mirror and always notice first the absent hair. In the future, every time I look in the mirror, before I see me, I'll see him first.

He takes out a knife and moves it back and forth.

Smells like fall, he says.

He puts my hair into his jacket pocket.

What if she finds it? I ask.

She won't.

He cups my face with his hands and kisses me.

I feel softer than I've felt for months, a feeling I'm a little uncomfortable with.

Overhead: birds.

#46

Purple irises surround the barn.
What terrible watchmen.
At least ten swallows
have taken up permanent residence.

And most disturbingly, I've seen
the ghost of my grandmother
counting bushels, worried there
won't be enough fruit to last
the family through the fall
and the months beyond.

#47

I climb the attic stairs with my notebook and pencil. Once up, I
sense the presence of moths.

A pillow is on the slanted plank by the window. I will sit there
and write, look outside through the dusty glass.

I look outside of myself. The pine trees are tired, the grass a
dirty rug.

I open my notebook to write but the paper feels too soft. I write
red on my skin. I write it again. Again.

I feel alive.

#49

Deep inside cold January
I can still see
the summer moonlight
on my skin.

Take a picture? I ask her.

Of what? she returns.

#50

We move north into the purple twilight covering the bowing wheat.

About the dress? I ask.

How many more times will I come to this field?

Yes, he says.

The silhouettes of tall pines grow darker.

I know, I say.

Hungry bats crawl out of my heart and go searching to feast.

#52

I'm in the dining room, giving birth. It wasn't planned but here
I am, on the table. It is dark outside and the chandelier is on
above me. I'm clinging to the warm light. There are women
and one man. The man is thick and has stubble on his face. The
stubble bothers me, even in the middle of all the pain.

The red walls are duller than the red that's coming out of
me. That red is the color of raspberry jam. It's bright and
announcing itself unabashedly. I can feel the stickiness of it
and want to tell everyone to eat, so I do. There's plenty. They
ignore me.

I am sweating and feel a bomb go off. And then another. The man
smiles. I concentrate on the light and land on top of it, brush
my wings against it.

My children leave at night and I let them.

I am a mother who understands the need to be untraceable.

Twins, I dream they've painted their boy faces similarly. Red sumac stains on their hands. Grinning, they are digging in the south orchard, two mirrors looking for arrowheads.

The moon is heavy and cocooning while they show each other
the quiet weapons, slip them into their pockets.

Their eyes look up at the house, worried I'll come running toward them.
But I roll over, let them dig until morning.

#59

I feel the storm coming so I dress for the occasion: a black slip
trimmed with lace. The first time in so long I've felt luxurious.

I light candles and slow dance, sway my hips.
The thunder a pulse thicker than mine, stronger.
I let it carry me, ride its echo.

I am following the pleasure of the storm until I'm inside of it.
The lightning entering my veins, running, diffusing. It's thrilling
how turned on I've become.

Who was it that told me not to be greedy? Who said
some sweetness is too deep?

I am the storm in my front porch and I am moving,
a threat to this home and everything in it.

#61

I cut my heart open. It's certain:
the meat of a halved dove still beating and bloody.
I've dreamed about her before.

In the dream she didn't look this delicious.

There's plenty to eat on this farm and yet
there's only me. Some things spoil.

I'll leave her out as an offering.
And then I'll watch, and wait.

#64

The tiger lilies' throats look so beautiful in the heat of noon. I want to slice them open. I want to chew them hungrily.

They remind me of the woman I love. Her white neck was always begging for the same treatment, but she died before I could slit her.

They say her hair caught fire, her whole body singed. This is why she stopped sending me letters: she is now ash. I wish she would have been more thoughtful.

This is why I'm not waiting on the lilies. Beautiful things are always moving towards ugliness. It's just a matter of who reaches them first.

When I chewed, I swallowed their seeds. Soon they will sprout, grow out my throat.

Who will be waiting with a knife for me?

#66

Morning snakes through the orchard. Young apricot trees
like wind chimes touch, then part. I wake on my belly
and into the loneliness stitched to my bones. I'm sore with it.

Wait, a voice says.

I do.

One, then two bodies. Gray pelts, running.

My bones soften when they find me.

The coyotes growl. Their teeth: yellowed, sharp.

#69

I've been dancing again at night in the orchard
underneath a key lime moon, the one you said looked wicked
just like me.

I'm embracing my darkness, which is just another way of saying
it was me that prayed for the death of certain relatives and it happened,
so maybe you were right.

#71

the breeze in summer
turns me on
at night
without covers
naked
sleeping
on the porch

outside
blossoms hum
under the spring
stars

are the dragonflies
also sleeping?

I dream
of her darkness
definite, expanding

when I wake
I still taste her
plum skin, her sour
sour heart.

#72

Here the only mountains are my elbows or my knees.
When I bend them just so I fall back in love with myself.

Thank goodness.

Eating blackberries is one way I've found to rid myself
of my wickedness. The sweetness transfers,
and I become the woman I've always wanted to be,
the one in a clean white dress standing on a shore, waving.

#77

On the lawn chairs we drink wine spritzer. Strawberries,
blackberries, mint, basil, rosé. We share a cigarette, pass it back
and forth. Our clouds evaporate quickly.

Lightning bugs hover above the grass. A blinking constellation
that we can touch.

The only way to catch lightning bugs is to pinch their bottoms off, you say.

No it's not, I say.

You put your glass down and walk into the stars. My stomach
knots as you head out.

Star killer, come back with glowing dust on your fingers.

#78

When it rains the walls breathe smoke signals: grandfather
gone but here.

The sunflowers, he begins, *did you plant them?*

Yes, I answer. *They're just shoots.*

*But I'm hopeful I'll see their bright faces soon
and bring them to you.*

#79

I wish someone would carry me
into the house, put me to bed
the place I've been longing to die
and let me. The truth is I go on forever.

Meet me in the apple orchard
look west, out over the ridge
and on any given night, watch me set.

#80

These bones are flowering. Do you smell them?

Yes, he says, *Pear blossoms.*

Exactly, I say. *What can we do
to make sure the young fruit
doesn't get eaten like last year
by the deer?*

Hope, he says.

That won't be enough.

#81

I am lying in the apple orchard again
waiting to turn invisible. I've been here for hours.

To be the clouds crawling through the blue sky
or the mice running in damp tunnels.

Here my body is heavy with salt.

I try to leave but it's impossible. My flesh reddening,
my freckles mapping where I begin, where I'll end.

#83

What's the sound of rain falling in my heart?
It's spring and I'm so goddamn curious, waking up green
every morning hoping to see a frog or some sign
I'll make it to summer.

I'm hopeful but I'm also realistic. Most days, in my pocket,
I carry a small, sharp knife.

I know when the coyotes howl they are hungry and hoping
to taste blood. They'll be coming soon and I want to give them
something, an offering, to prove to them just how kind I can be.

#84

Autumn enters my blood early
and I let it. Soon it will be wine.

Who would like to drink me
underneath the harvest moon?

#87

I wake up inside my dress. Something is moving underneath the dirty lace. It feels wet and dark. It might be the river.

I get out of bed and pull on my sweater. It doesn't smell like him anymore. There's no need to be quiet. He took the twins months ago. No one is sleeping in this house.

Down the stairs and outside are the forest and the moon. The moon's light reaches the daffodils, turns them honeydew. They glow, light the way to the river.

At the river I look into the dark water. The fish are sleeping while the current carries them to the lake.

I scratch my skin. Blood sprouts and blooms slowly. I put my tongue to it. It's sweet like black raspberries. I want to sleep, to be carried.

#90

It's a nightgown because it has seen the moon,
but I wear it all day. My hair long
and rough, like the bark of the apple tree in the front yard.

I hear my father climbing. He is not afraid of falling.
On the ground, the bees are busy eating fruit.

If I leave this farm, I'll braid my hair tightly,
tie the ends with pink satin ribbons. I'll go quietly
and plan to never return.

#93

Everything is not exactly as it seems. In this country,
I am not bound here by blood or bone.

Each time I think of leaving a new hole appears
on the thick clovered lawn.

By mid-August, a collection of underground caves
lined with jacketed bodies buzzing: a hunger
that sounds deeper than any I've ever known.

They've told me they know my scent and they'll find me.
They've told me if I try to leave,
it wouldn't take them too long.

I believe them and stay for centuries.

#94

My blood? I've fed it to the turtles, to the berries
to anything hungry and wanting. All you had to do
was ask.

I always had what you wanted, didn't I?

#95

I dream of the minnows in the lake: a fast cloud moving against
the sand. They never sink but I do.

Everything is water
even you, even me.

I write her a note with clouds
traveling slower than minnows.

I know she'll receive this message.
I choose to believe she'll be here soon.

#98

It is July and the dandelion seeds are spreading.
Everywhere I step, beliefs I planted
have rooted:

I don't belong on the ground.

I am more than body.

The wind, when I hear it singing, it's me telling myself

something sweet and something sacred.

#100

I can hear things coming to an end. The feathers of birds flying south. The half eaten leaves of plants. The pods, pregnant with seed.

I press my thumb and forefinger into a milkweed sack and they enter, swim inside the dry belly of silk. I pinch and catch the hairs between my fingertips.

I pull the silk out and put the small clump to my lips. Brush right to left. I let go and watch the wisps lift and carry, scatter.

The wind is everywhere and so everything moves. It's hard to see past my thick, swirling hair. Everything impossible to track.

#101

The mirror of my heart is
reflecting fields of wild
flowers that grew in after we
stopped tending to
the asparagus.

Look what comes
of letting go:
perfuming chaos
complete with butterflies
and a warm, summer
breeze.

#103

In October I do not know which is which:
the iridescent hanging plum is my heart.
I am tired but not yet ready for winter, so I go wandering.

Along the unkempt edges of the orchards,
the black raspberries grow wildly.
They cut into my flesh in several places.

The cuts immediately fill with petals, soft and white:
a churning wave of blossoms.

I walk with a new tenderness.

Soon the wind will blow the petals: a blizzard of flowers.
Burning red, the scar where the blossoms once held, hoping to
    bear fruit.
I lick it and it's sweet.

#107

The black birds are circling again and I haven't slept in weeks.

The color underneath my eyes: smudged blackberries.

I can't remember; was it me that smeared this fruit on my body during fall?

#112

It is midnight. The moon is a hardboiled egg in the sky.

I walk to the pool that is covered with leaves. Even with the light, the water is black.

I know where the tadpoles live. My hair dips into the water when I reach my hand in. I scoop up some dark matter. Several small bodies are wiggling.

They are slimy and cold. They are spotted. I know I could squeeze them to their deaths.

I make a fist but loosely, flex my palm towards the sky, let the bodies slip back into the water.

I lower myself into the river, open my eyes.

Here the moonlight is an echo. Here the moonlight is the loveliest.

#114

We are standing in a navy blue forest and I'm sweating.

She smiles.

A row of gold teeth twist out of her upper jaw.

I'm looking for the blue heron, she says, unconvincingly. *Have you seen him?*

In her right hand, my aunt carries a knife. The blade, made out of
pearl or bone, glows.

I go to scream and begin coughing.

She laughs. *I thought I'd make us a stew.*

Gray feathers exit my mouth hurriedly. She collects them calmly.

She licks her blade and asks, *You know how much I love you, don't you?*

#117

An old lover said to me, *A rose is a nice way*
to remind the person you love about impermanence.

I pick a yellow one and stuff it into an envelope
send it to the person who thought they could leave me
and yet.

#120

In the afternoon, I show her how to plant radish.
We scatter seed, cover them lightly with dark soil.

She leaves and forgets me.

When the radish sprout I can't help myself; I think of her skin, pull one
out of the ground.

I slice it thickly, eat the radish with butter on toast
at breakfast. I drink coffee to wash it down.

#124

Life how
fleeting
and yet the field
filled with sweet
scented bright bombs
so many wild flowers
blooming even now

the mind has a way
of remembering explosions
especially when
they continue
to go off inside
a beating
heart

#127

My parents died years ago but they are still with me. On the porch I
 write them this letter, while outside the fig leaves spill rainwater:

Dear Mom,
Dear Dad,

I picked the wild flowers.
They weren't enough.

I leave the letter on the stack I've already written.

They always write back.

#128

your eyes
blackberry blossoms
hundreds of them
soft and delicate white
pulsing in the moon
I feel safe with you watching

what strange
animal could harm me
while you're present?

I stay out
past midnight
walk
the field
my feet sinking
into cold sand

in morning what new
message will I
have written?

#130

My smile —
the moon
he never looks
up to see
all of this
bright milk
and oh
is it
sweet!

#131

Leaves litter the orchard. They are brown and sun dried. Sand
sticks to their bellies.

I lift one and inhale. It is a place I keep forgetting.
It is a place I don't want to forget.

I rub the leaf with my fingers and it fractures, falls easily.
Leaves no stain on my skin.

#134

The tomatoes look just like me
swollen and holey
ants crawling in and out of every
crevice, taking what they need.

I am looking at the sun waiting
as my insides feed hundreds of mouths.

This skin, sun stained, perfuming. Will the birds
come for what's left of me and how far from here
will they take me?

Let it be far and let it be soon.

#27 is for Nobuko Kimura

#59 is for Bobbi Jene Smith

●●●●●● Acknowledgments

THANK YOU TO the editors of the following journals and magazines where these poems, and earlier versions of them, first appeared: *Pinwheel, Queen Mob's Tea House, Phantom Books, Tinderbox Poetry Journal, Banango Street, Vending Machine Press, Gramma Poetry,* and *Hobart.*

"#90" and "#103" first appeared in *Michigan Quarterly Review.*

"#59," "#61," "#81," and "#94" were September's featured poems on *The Rumpus.*

"#22" was first published in Aaron Stern & Jordan Sullivan's *Dialogues 02: 52 Photographs & 25 Poems* (New York: 205-A, 2016).

A resounding thank you to everyone at Wayne State University Press.

Immense gratitude to my friends and mentors who have been a consistent source of encouragement and inspiration, especially: Sari Adelson, Mary-Kim Arnold, Gina Bonati, Eileen Cropley, GloATL movement artists, Erika L. Sánchez, Zachary Swisher, Robert James Russell, and Keith Taylor.

Thank you forever to my family, and everything at 3459 and 327.

About the Author

ELIZABETH SCHMUHL IS a multidisciplinary artist whose work appears in *Michigan Quarterly Review*, *The Rumpus*, *Paper Darts*, *PANK*, *Hobart*, *Pinwheel*, and elsewhere. She has worked at various nonprofits, including the John F. Kennedy Center for Performing Arts, and currently works at the University of Michigan, Ann Arbor.